A Jonah Day

The Story of Jonah and a Very Big Fish

Written and illustrated by
Phil A. Smouse

The Lord's word to Jonah came quite unexpected:
"Go down to Nineveh. You've been elected.
Tell all the people there, without delay,
this thing that I tell you to tell them today."

"Nineveh! Goodness! Of all of the places!
Those Ninevites all have the *nastiest* faces.
They're rude and they're crude and I'd have to conclude
they're an ill-tempered brood of the *worst* magnitude.

But I guess that I'll do it.
It is on my way.
Now *what* is it, Lord, that You want me to say?"

"*THUS SAYS THE LORD! This is what you should say:*
'Listen up, or I may have to ruin your day!

You're all mean, and you're nasty and not very nice,
and those are your GOOD points, to be more precise.
For I mean what I say, and I am quite sincere
when I tell you I smell you the whole way up here!'"

"Tell *that* to *them*? You must be mistaken!
You certainly can't expect *me* to partake in
a dreadful, impossible scheme," Jonah spat,
"like the one you're suggesting and that, Lord, is *that!*"

"How awful, how shocking, how horribly harsh-ish!"
he thought as he boarded a boat bound for Tarshish.
And down in the very most bottomest part
Jonah laid there alone, just himself and his heart.

Jonah laid in that boat, and he thought and he thought;
but he just couldn't do what he knew that he ought.
Now, you can't run away from the Lord. Jonah knew it,
but he was about to find out what occurs when you DO it!

The weather started getting rough.
The tiny ship was tossed. . .

A tempest blew. The crewmen flew!
The thunder boomed. "We're surely doomed!"
they all presumed, "to be consumed here
by this holocaust!"

"All hands on deck, all hands on deck!"
the captain shouted out.

"And Jonah, *you*
get up here too!

Because,
if I am not mistaken,
this earthquaking
is the making
of the likes
of YOU."

The crew drew straws to figure out
just who should be ejected
for causing this calamity
to which they'd been subjected.

The shortest straw would tell them who,
and as he had predicted, the captain watched
with no surprise. . .

as good old Jonah picked it!

"Okay, okay, it's all my fault.
Just throw me out. The storm will stop!"

"You heard the man. Let's throw him in!"
the sailors shouted with a grin.
"Yes, bon voyage and tally-ho,
let's pick him up and heave him, HO!"

"Wait a minute. Not so fast,"
the captain shouted, flabber-gassed.
"Let's try again. Let's make the shore.
Now grab your oars and row some more.

Stroke,
stroke,
stroke,
stroke!"

But they simply couldn't do it. . .

So they threw him out in-TO it!

And, all at once, the thunder stopped.
The sea grew calm.
The sun came out.

What God did Jonah so betray
to cause this startling display
where even wind
and waves obey?

(Now deeper and deeper he found himself sinking,
which prompted old Jonah to do some rethinking!)

"Oh Lord," Jonah cried, "have you left me for dead?
The waves and the waters encircle my head.
Barnacles clutch at my fingers and toes,
and some wet, wiggly thing is attached to my nose!

Oh, there's nothing, I'm sure, quite so dreadful as this. . ."

"Except being swallowed alive by a fish!"

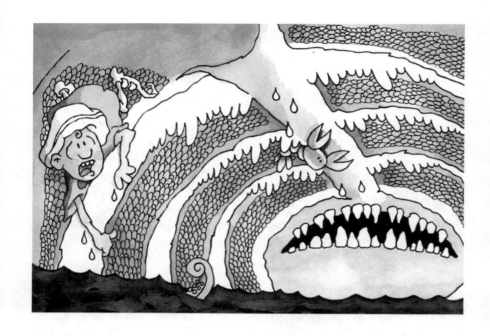

"Inside of a fish! Oh, of all of the places!
Of all of the dreadful, disgraceful disgraces!
I'll do what you ask, Lord! I'll do it your way.
I'll do it right now, right this minute, today."

So that fish spat up Jonah right there on the beach;
and the minute it did, Jonah started to preach.

"'Forty more days, says the Lord. It's a fact.
You've got forty short days left to clean up your act.

For you're mean, and you're nasty and not very nice;
And those are your good points, to be more precise.
Yes, I mean what I say and I am quite sincere
when I tell you I smell you the whole way up here!'"

Now, everyone there from the king straight on down
was convinced that this guy wasn't fooling around.

So they cleaned up their hearts.
Yes, they cleaned up their act.
And they cleaned it up quick,
as a matter of fact. . . .

But forty days passed, and then forty-one,
and the Lord didn't do what He said would be done.

"Lord, what's going on here? I look like a goof.
You said you'd destroy them.
Now give me some proof!"

"Proof, my friend Jonah? You don't understand.
All of creation is at my command!

And no matter how angry or hurtful or mean,
unfaithful, unworthy or selfish you've been,
I'll never reject you or turn you away.
For I love you so deeply, I barely can say."